Autism and Falling in Love

To the One That Got Away

Kerry Magro M.A.

ISBN: 0692338098

ISBN-13: 978-0692338094

DEDICATION

This book is dedicated to my friends, family, the one that got away and our autism community. I'll always be grateful for all of you!

DISCLAIMER

Some facts from this book have been changed and left out to protect the privacy of the people involved with this book and story.

CONTENTS

ACKNOWLEDGMENTS

I would like to acknowledge that this is my personal reflection upon one of the most amazing years of my life. Hopefully it will help me to grow into the partner I will be for someone in the future. I wish for happiness for the person who shared this experience with me, and am grateful for everyone in my life...

INTRODUCTION

What would you do for the people in your life that you love?

In a society where nearly half of all marriages end in divorce and relationships fall apart every day, it seems difficult for people to fight to keep the people they love in their lives...

Throw in the word "autism" and things like relationships can seem impossible. Autism is defined as a social and communication disorder that affects over three million individuals and counting in the United States today.

One thing I wanted to share with you before we dig deeper is a stigma I hope we can erase through this book and that is....

People with autism can't feel empathy or love...

Some of the most passionate people I know today are young adults who happen to be on the autism spectrum. While some of the main characteristics of autism involve social difficulties, a lot of the time people with autism are stereotyped as not wanting relationships and want to be left alone.

But in all reality, many with autism can feel empathy, they can feel love, and because they are usually able to think critically and consciously have some of the biggest hearts out of anyone you will ever meet. Although the spectrum is wide and every person you meet with autism is unique, many are completely authentic, genuine and sincere.

This is where my story begins. When I was four I was diagnosed with autism. Growing up I couldn't communicate verbally. My behaviors in school related to my autism resulted in me being asked to leave multiple schools. When I did start speaking, no one wanted to be my friend because even when I did start communicating, I was at a disadvantage compared to my peers. During this time no one knew what my future would be.

Thanks to working around the clock, making autism my 24/7 job between my services and the support of my family I was able to overcome many of my obstacles. Because to countless hours of occupational, physical and speech therapy, I now have a full time job, live independently and have been in romantic relationships.

I had a normal situation in high school when it came to finding success in relationships. For most kids on the autism spectrum I know that can often be difficult.

My first relationship started when I was 18. I was varsity captain of my high school basketball team and she was a varsity cheerleader. It was really one of those storybook type of relationships that you see in the movies.

About a year later, after we had both graduated, I told her that we should get married. Although I never really mentioned this notion to my family or friends, it definitely felt real to me at the time. This was going to be the girl I started a life with.

As we both left for two different colleges, things started to change in our relationship.

The transition to college was a difficult one for me as I was living on campus and away from home for the first time. I became a part of several school groups and was heavily involved in an honors program, which didn't give me a lot of time to focus on having a girlfriend. Four months into my freshman year, we broke up…and my heart was broken for the first time.

It's true what they say about the first break up being the hardest. I loved that girl and saw her in my future, but going the distance wasn't in the cards.

For the rest of my college experience (which lasted six years between getting a Bachelor's degree in Business Administration/Sports Management and a Master's degree in Strategic Communication, both at Seton Hall University) I began to adapt splinter skills to deal with my social relationships. I was always involved in social groups and that substituted me trying to get into any serious relationships while I was focused on school and my activities.

This didn't mean I didn't have any relationships. I had several "flings" and two more relationships with two incredible women during my college years. This was the perfect situation for me. For the most part I avoided my deepest fear since I was a child: BEING ALONE.

After graduating and beginning my search to find a full time job and become a "full-time adult" so to speak, I met the one that got away. She was my fourth girlfriend and the second woman I fell in love with. Out of all of my relationships there was something different about her. Not only was she beautiful, but she also had a beautiful heart. She had the most amazing brown eyes which matched her hair.

It became clear to me right away that she was as beautiful on the inside as she was on the outside. I had never met someone like her before and when I lost her I had to take a good look at myself and understand why things happened the way they did.

Within the first 24 hours I had some thoughts on what could have happened but not a clear-cut understanding. When I finally talked to her about what went wrong, I was in a really bad place. Within an hour of that conversation, I started seeking out help, buying books on Amazon on how to be a better partner in a relationship and finding books on autism and relationships to give me a better perspective.

I was diagnosed with autism when I was four, and in past relationships I've been called self-centered and not understanding of other's perspectives. As much as I've worked on it and tried to better myself, it has remained a challenge for me.

This time around though, I knew I had to make a drastic change. So while seeking help, reading as much as I could on the subject and talking to friends and family about what had gone wrong I just kept thinking about what I'd do with a second chance. What I'd do to have 30 minutes to show her what I have been working on to not only improve as a partner but as a person.

In my first book I wrote "Defining Autism From The Heart" I shared a poem titled "My Name is Kerry and I Have PDD-NOS". The poem read...

My name is Kerry and I have Pervasive Developmental Disorder- Not Otherwise Specified.

This means I have autism.

This does not mean I *am* autism.

This means I see the world sometimes in a different light.

This does not mean I'm in the dark.

This means from time to time I may have a difficulty expressing my emotions.

This does not mean I don't feel.

This means when I communicate, I do it with a style that is my own.

This does not mean I don't have a voice.

This means I may have sensitivity when it comes to a certain feel or touch.

This means I can often focus on certain interests for a long period of time.

This does not mean those are my only interests.

This means that I'm the only person in my family to have this.

This does not mean I'm alone.

This means I may have 500 other symptoms/capabilities that are different than yours.

This does not mean I'm any less of a person than you are.

My name is Kerry, and regardless of what PDD-NOS means or doesn't mean, autism can't define me, and I define autism. I can only hope those individuals, regardless of being autistic or not can define their lives and their journeys in the way they see it.

After overcoming obstacles to get where I am today I've now come to understand instead of defining the obstacles that made me struggle growing up, now as an adult I want to define how to become a better partner for the people I care for. I want to be the type of guy who loves unconditionally and can show that consistently every day.

This is how the book came about. Part I of this book is my personal story, in Part II you will learn more about autism and relationships and in Part III as an adult with autism writing this book I will give you resources on how you can be a better partner to the people you care for. I hope by using the resources in Part III you will be better prepared to have relationships.

I've wanted to write a book about autism and relationships since I was 19 and now, seven years later, I want to write a book about one of the most amazing people I've ever met.

At the end of the day, as cliché as it may sound, I want to be better for her because I know how lucky I was to have her in my life. Now that I have realized this, I want to show her. Regardless if I never hear from her or see her again that she'll always hold a special place in my life because of what we shared.

THE SIGNIFICANCE OF A SUNFLOWER

In the writing of this many people who have taken the time to read the book have asked me questions along the lines of, "Kerry, could you have come out with a manlier book cover" in reference to the sunflower...

The significance of a sunflower has a huge role in the inspiration of this book. The first time I ever surprised the woman who inspired this book, I gave her a sunflower because I knew those were her favorites. I remember her reaction when she told me about how the delivery man was beating on her door and how she was like, "who the hell is banging?" until she realized the flowers were from me.

The weekend I told her I loved her for the first time I also got her sunflowers because I wanted her to feel as special and as cared for as possible when I told her.

In many ways she depicted a lot of similar qualities to a sunflower. Specifically, this woman had a very warm heart.

Since she was the inspiration of the book I sought out a cover that would give her a sunflower one more time...

PART I: TO THE ONE THAT GOT AWAY

"A man must be big enough to admit his mistakes, smart enough to profit from them, and strong enough to correct them." — John C. Maxwell

To The One That Got Away,

When I finish writing this letter to you this could very well be the last time I'll ever get to communicate with you again and that's what makes writing this book one of the hardest and most important things I'll ever do.

I'm not sure if you'll ever read this, but there are so many things I regret that happened between us. One thing I will never regret though is meeting you. The one thing I thought of our relationship more than anything was something you said to me once. Over just a short period of time you became my best friend and my heart.

When the breakup happened and you mentioned what had gone wrong, I began to seek out help to figure out how I could get you back in my life. I began working on how to become a better partner. I started reading books on relationships and putting in the hours to try to grasp things better.

I worked on myself harder than I ever had before. What could I do that I wasn't doing already to improve myself to make you see that things could be better? I started seeking help on what I could do to fix what had gone wrong in the relationship. I was determined, and during this time I learned a lot about myself in the process. I wanted a clean slate with you, but first I wanted to make sure I did right by you and learned the lessons I needed to gain your trust again.

One of those lessons was about understanding you as a person. In relationships, you can't control others; you can only control your own actions. My logic was flawed. My obstacle wasn't supposed to be how to convince you to get back together with me, but how to understand things from your perspective so I could understand why things went the way they did. You can't force people into thinking things will change; you have to show them through your actions.

When it came to perspective, I really tried to put myself in your shoes during this time. When I replayed parts of the relationship in my head I began to realize the damage I was doing. I may have not seen it fully at the time but it's pretty obvious to me now. That's not the person I ever wanted to come off as or be, especially towards someone I care about as much as I care about you.

With all of this going on over the past few months I've really had to take a hard look at myself and think about who I am as a person. Mainly, I had to look at what I had done wrong to lose you. Now that we aren't together anymore I keep thinking to myself about how I lost one of the best things that's ever happened to me. When I told you I was blind by many of the things I did I truly was. Even now I still look at things and tell myself all of the things I would do to have a second chance with you. When I lost you, it felt like I lost a family member. I was pushing you so hard to try to convince you to get back with me when I should have been trying to work on myself.

I have always tried to live a life in self-reflection and I think because of this, I've become very self-aware but not aware of others' needs.

It doesn't justify things. Although there were things that went wrong there were still so many things I loved about our relationship. When I told you I was willing to fight for us that's the reason why I was willing too.

I remember when it all started during Autism Awareness Month last April. It was a day that I will remember for the rest of my life. That was the day I met you. I remember seeing you in the audience several times while I was giving my talk and was really happy when you came up to me afterwards, asking to take a photo with me. When you messaged me after the talk was over and wanted to start a school group, I was really touched by how much you cared about the autism community. This was the first time I got to see how big your heart was. I wasn't sure what was going to happen but I knew you seemed like such a genuinely sweet person who I wanted to get to know.

As we started to get to know each other better through messaging I loved how we would go back and forth about fun facts between the two of us. I still remember one of the first fun facts you mentioned to me. I just kept thinking to myself how inaccurate that was. When you tagged me in the post all my coworkers kept asking me about who the cute girl is taking a selfie with my book. I also loved teasing you because of your fear of ketchup and that we both were, without even knowing it, at the Backstreet Boys Millennium Tour Concert in 1999 in New Jersey.

When we finally had our first date I was extremely nervous. When we got to the restaurant and neither of us had any idea what to eat because everything was super fancy/expensive it was hilarious to see our reactions. The best moment I had with you I think on that entire date was when we just hung out in my car talking. We must have been in that parking lot for over an hour. Than one of the best moments happened in our relationship when I got to hold your hand for the first time because you blushed and turned away. It was honestly one of the most adorable things I've ever seen.

I think that was just a theme about the entire time we were together. I was just so happy with you. When the sunset and we went back outside on that first date, I loved holding your hand. I still remember us trying to take our first selfie together and we couldn't figure out how to work the flash in the dark. I just remember us both freezing but looking at the New York skyline while I hugged you and stared out at the lights with you. You were shivering and I just wanted to hold you close. When I dropped you off after that date and you hugged me before leaving I knew this could be the start of something special.

Then we met together to do a walk for autism and I introduced you to my community. I was so glad I had you there with me. I loved holding your hand during that entire walk. When we went to get pancakes after the walk and I asked you to be my girlfriend it was one of the better moments of my life. I remember how excited we were about going "official" on Facebook and how we were stunned by the amount of likes we got on that status.

One of the best moments I had when we were together

was when we played card games with someone special in your family during Fourth of July weekend. She instantly got the nickname of my mini BFF (even though she was clearly cheating to help you win). She grew on me and it also opened another side of me to you. I saw the love you had for her and you became even that more amazing to me. You care about others so much and I found that so attractive about you.

Than we had our weekend in my hometown together where we watched "The Notebook," had frozen yogurt, and even ended up going to a random WNBA game at Madison Square Garden. Out of all of our times together this one will always stand out to me because this was the first time I told you I loved you. You were the first woman I trusted with my heart in more than seven years. When you said you loved me back and told me the first time you fell in love with me…it was a weekend I never wanted to end.

The day I lost you was one of the most difficult days of my life. I was heartbroken. I was upset. I was confused and didn't really understand what the problem was. I know there were a few issues but it was so sudden. My entire body was in a sense of shock and because of that I ended up having a panic attack for the first time in my life that night. The next day I woke up again and had another panic attack. I saw a doctor that day to get some medication to help with the stress and to help me sleep.

The second day on the medicine I had a negative reaction to it and ended up in the emergency room with shakes and my third panic attack in four days.

I was a mess and definitely hit one of the lowest points I had in a long time. While in my head I knew everything was going to be alright, my body was shutting down on me. The coping strategies I had used my previous relationships weren't working. It became even clearer to me then how much I really cared for you.

When we broke up, I was just thinking to myself what I would have done to try to get us to last until your birthday weekend and then for the weekends after. Maybe then I could have made things better to the point where we would still be together.

For your birthday I got us on a dinner cruise on the Hudson River Saturday night and a matinee to see Wicked on Broadway Sunday. During our dinner on Sunday night after Wicked was when I was going to give you the big surprise. After you saw Luke Bryan in concert who I met at The NASCAR FedEx 400 Benefiting Autism Speaks last spring I came up with the idea to try to find a way to get him to record an mp3 to sing happy birthday to you. When that didn't work I found a way to get backstage passes for us see him at Madison Square Garden in the middle of September. I wanted to make your birthday amazing but more importantly, after all of the surprises you gave me during our relationship I wanted to give you one that would make you the happiest I've ever seen you...

I was really touched when your family reached out to me after the breakup to make sure that I was doing ok. We both know how much I care for someone special in your family. I still remember that drawing they did of us that they created based off that selfie we took together. I also still have that cute collage they did with my first book.

I know this might not mean much but even if we never see each other again I want to leave thinking that some good could have come out of our relationship. The reason I wrote this book is because of how much I loved you and wanted the world to know how incredible you are and hopefully help others understand the importance of loving the ones in their lives to the fullest.

Receiving a monetary gain from this book was never my intention. I plan on donating 50% of the proceeds from this book to Best Buddies and 50% of the proceeds to Autism Speaks: two organizations we are both passionate about.

Because of you and the other 500 some odd awesome intangibles you brought to our relationship, I wanted to say thank you. Because of you, I've realized the standard

I want for my future relationships. If I've learned anything from this, it's that mistakes have consequences. This is one of the bigger consequences I will ever have to live with. I hope from this experience, however, that I can come back stronger. As we move on, I just wanted you to know you are one of the most incredible people I've ever met.

Even now, in the back of my mind, I still regret the mistakes I've made. It's true what they say about not knowing a good thing until it's gone. Of all of the relationships I've had, ours was, by far, the one that meant the most. It's still obvious to me how special you are.

I've never tried so hard to make myself better for anyone in my past. If I'm ever lucky enough again to have a woman as incredible as you in my life, I'm going to make it my mission to make sure she is treated like a queen and is loved and respected.

I know I can't change the past and I wish I could. I've never regretted anything more in my entire life. I wanted to make amends with you, and also make amends to your friends and family to let them know how sorry I was if this situation affected them in anyway.

I would write a book to make things right with us; I'd seek out help to make things right with us. I'd do it to make things work for us. We had a good thing going. When you love someone you have to work at it. One of my close friends and I had a conversation about this after you told me what had gone wrong. I told him how I was blind to many of the things I did and how I'd do anything to get things back to where they were.

My friend's response was simple, "If you love someone then you have to show them what you're willing to do for them when things are at the lowest point. Anyone can say they love someone but words can only do so much. If you want her back, than show her you're worth a second chance."

I've learned a great deal from losing you. I've realized for one how important communication is in any relationship. I think we both misunderstood each other a lot at times and I wish we could have talked about things more to make sure we both felt comfortable in the relationship. I never meant to hurt you. As a kid, having a certified communication disorder I had to go through hours of therapy to learn how to communicate properly. That's why when you said you were hoping the issues that occurred in our relationship would pass I became defensive. I didn't put in enough of an effort to communicate with you to make sure things were going right and I regret that.

I really wish I saw things more clearly from the start. I should have been better at understanding. I thought things were ok and if I knew they weren't, I would have worked at it while we were together.

You explained so much of your past to me and I didn't do a good enough job of explaining my past to you.

Looking back I wish I explained more of my difficulties to you about myself so you could have better understood why certain situations went the way they did. For example, my sensory issues have always been a challenge for me. Things that bothered you like having to have a fan on bothered me because of the noise. I wish I had told you that.

Other things like mind blindness and transitions have always been a struggle for me. That's why not understanding things like personal space in relationships has always been difficult for me. I also have a hypersensitivity to both physical and emotional pain. Emotional pain can be unbearable at times; when there's a lot going on I could feel like things are going into overload for me. I always keep a straight face in public but it's still a challenge for me. Along with losing you the pain I felt was awful because I thought I had hurt you. I never felt guiltier about losing someone in my entire life.

It's something I've been working on to this day. I wish I could show you now. When I was in college my best friend and I stopped speaking for several weeks because of some issues that arose. When we finally had a chance to sit down and talk about where things went wrong I took out a piece of paper and wrote down all of the problems with a bullet listed under each one of the ways I was going to work on them to make things right.

I did the same thing with us when we broke up. I wrote down the list and what I could do to fix it. That's when I started seeking help.

I misunderstood you and I'm sorry for that. I hope you realize that if we both had communicated with each other about the issues before breaking up, I would have done the same stuff I'm doing now. I've seen so many relationships crash and burn because of a lack of communication. I've always believed that relationships take a ton of work. I don't think we ever gave each other that chance to work on things. Looking back, you had every right to be upset. I didn't give you enough space because along with everything else I couldn't help but think I was about to lose one of the best things that's ever happened to me.

Your emotions and how you were feeling were completely valid. I know we've both had a difficult time trusting people from our pasts and I could understand you wanting to push away. It was unfair of me to say I could change so soon after the breakup. I was showing a lack of maturity, trying to self-validate myself and putting my needs ahead of your own. In the end though, I'd change and be better for you because the alternative of never having you in my life again was something I never wanted to face.

At the end of the day after time has passed all I know is that I still love you as much as I did when I first told you that this summer. These past few months of not having you in my life have been some of the most difficult months of my life. We had so many amazing times and I wish that could have happened in the future. In my past I've been seen as a jerk but I never knew that was jeopardizing what we had.

That speaking event in April will always mean the most to me because I met you. It's given me a whole new appreciation for what I do with my speaking career because of it. It has taught me that you really never know who you are going to meet in your life and that you should always be open to the opportunities that are present for yourself.

I never stopped caring for you. I wish I didn't have to spend another minute trying to get over you. I wanted to be there for you for all of the stuff you had going on in your life. I wanted to be there for you in your future and help show you love when you became one of the very best in your profession because of your heart. I wanted to be there to help your awesome family member aka my mini-BFF as they go through school. I wanted to be there to do hibachi with your family and still have one of your favorite men in your life as part of 'Kerry's Army'. AND I wanted to be there when I finally found a way to get you to meet Luke Bryan to see your reaction when you freaked out and tried to convince him to marry you.

When someone in your family wrote a review of my book and said I was "going places" I thought to myself that I was going places because I finally had it all: A great job, great friends, great family and a woman who had every single piece of my heart.

As I'm writing this, I really wish I could share your name for whoever ends up reading this to share with them how amazing you are. So for whatever employer gets a hold of this book would hire you on the spot because they would know how incredible you are. When I went to meet Temple Grandin for the first time this summer and I got you an autographed copy of her book "The Autistic Brain," I was telling her about you and how much you meant to me, I thought how you could have the same impact in your future one day that she has had in the autism community. I really mean that. I hear so many stories about bullying and how ignorant some people are especially among individuals with special needs. I then look at you and I think about how much everyone is going to appreciate you. Your heart and what you are going to be able to do for whoever is lucky enough to snatch you up is going to mean the world to them.

I won't waste any more time in saying this but you already know how thankful I am for the time I had with you. When you look back at us I hope you remember the amazing times we had as a couple because, as much as there were things that went wrong, there was so much I think we loved about what we had together.

I wish I could go back to that day when I met you in April. How I could have changed the things I did wrong and given you a relationship where I promised to always communicate with you and work on the things needed like I'm doing now. That's what you've always deserved and no matter how much time passes I'm always going to care for you. As much as I move on your face still comes into my head anytime a John Legend song plays on the radio. The pain is still there and because of it everyday I'm working on being better. I am learning from my mistakes so hopefully one day when the pain stops I'll never have to go through these feelings again. You've given me some of the better days of my life and also some of the greatest lessons I'll ever have to learn.

I'm so grateful to you for that…

I wrote this in my last letter to you but please never change. You fell for me all that time ago and than I fell for you and whoever falls for you now is extremely lucky. You deserve the best and I'm sorry I couldn't give that to you when we were together. I tried to pour every bit of my heart and soul into this book because that's what I should have been giving you everyday we were together.

I didn't know how I wanted to end this letter because it might be the last time I would get to communicate with you. When that happened I started looking up songs for inspiration. I was inspired by one song from someone you love that made me feel exactly how I feel for you right now. So all I have left to say is…

I'm sorry for the past and I wish I could love you now like a story with a happy ending...

If you've ever loved someone, I hope you can relate to my story. For those reading this, regardless if you have autism or not, try to learn from my mistakes by trying to make a conscious effort to see things from your significant others' perspectives. Every relationship is about that bond between the two of you. It's easy sometimes to get lost in only thinking about your own needs but when that happens, you ignore your partner. Learn to invest in the people who mean the most to you. Respect and care for them because trust me, your relationships will be far better for it.

You make me want to hold you like a hammock
on a summer day
Tell you how I'm gonna take your cares away
You make me want to
You make me want to roll down the river and
around the bend
Love you like a story with a happy ending
You make me want to

I don't know if I can ever change
But you make me want to
You make me want to

Well I never met a girl like you
That's got me thinking like I do
To hang up my hat and kick off my boots
But you make me want to
You make me want to

You make me want to
Baby you make me want to
~ Luke Bryan (You Make Me Want To)

LOOKING BACK AT THE PAST YEAR…

During and since the time of the relationship I've had a lot of high points which has made this one of the best years of my life….

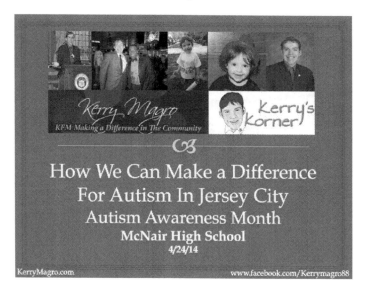

McNair is my in district high school and has always had a special meaning for me. McNair currently has a high school program for students with autism up to age 21. Each April I return there to speak to the students, teachers and paraprofessionals to offer them my perspective and resources of what it is like to live on the spectrum

STOCK EXCHANGE APPEARANCE

I graduated from Stillman School of Business and many of my classmates would love to be on the floor of the NYSE/Euronext. I have been lucky enough to be there several times with autism families ringing the Opening Bell on April 2nd World Autism Day, and this night raising funds for a remarkable high school in New Jersey, the Newmark School.

AUTISM AWARENESS EVENT AT CITIFIELD

Major league baseball has partnered to raise money and offer autism friendly experiences at ball parks around the country for those with autism. I had the opportunity to cover one of these games.

KEYNOTE SPEAKER AT MILLBURN HIGH SCHOOL IN MILLBURN, NEW JERSEY

All over the country Students are raising awareness of Autism in their community. This was a very special group of high school students who invited me to talk to them, their families and teachers.

GUEST SPEAKER AT NORTH CENTRAL NEW
JERSEY WALK NOW FOR AUTISM SPEAKS AT
METLIFE STADIUM IN EAST RUTHERFORD, NEW
JERSEY

I finally made it onto the field at MetLife Stadium
Rutherford NJ. Here I am speaking to encourage
our walkers for their great awareness and
fundraising efforts.

KEYNOTE SPEAKER AT MARION ELEMENTARY SCHOOL IN SHELBY, NORTH CAROLINA

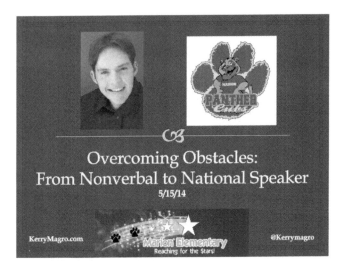

I had several great trips around the country this year. Here in a whirl wind tour I met and spoke to middle grade students, paraprofessionals and parents – each from a different perspective. Marion Middle School rocks!

COVERED THE NASCAR FEDEX 400 BENEFITING
AUTISM SPEAKS IN DOVER DELAWARE (I GOT
TO MEET COUNTRY STAR LUKE BRYAN AT THE
EVENT)

KEYNOTE SPEAKER AT THE 2ND ANNUAL MIDSOUTH AUTISM CONFERENCE IN MEMPHIS UNVERSITY IN MEMPHIS TENNESSEE.

BREAKOUT PRESENTER AT THE AUTISM
SOCIETY'S 45TH ANNUAL CONFERENCE AT THE
INDIANA CONVENTION CENTER IN
INDIANAPOLIS

KEYNOTE SPEAKER AT THE 2ND ANNUAL TEDXJERSEYCITY CONFERENCE IN JERSEY CITY, NEW JERSEY

RECEIVED THE MOST VOTES IN THE "30 UNDER
30 CAMPAIGN" RECOGNIZING
ENTREPRENUERS ON THE AUTISM SPECTRUM
UNDER THE AGE OF 30.

One of my projects I received amazing support on
from my friends was winning the '30 Under 30
Campaign' which highlights individuals with autism
under the age of 30. I received the most votes out
of the finalists in 2014 to help win a business grant
to help my non-profit KFM Making A Difference.

WORKED AT THE GOLDEN DOOR FILM
FESTIVAL IN JERSEY CITY, NEW JERSEY, FOR
AUTISM SPEAKS WHERE I GOT TO MEET
FASHION DESIGNER TOMMY HILFIGER.

The Golden Door Festival ran an Autism
Awareness series with lectures at Sensory Kids
LLC located in Jersey City. It was a great honor for
my hometown to host such an important event.

.

KEYNOTE PRESENTER AT J.P MORGAN CHASE
IN NEW YORK CITY

Employers like J.P. Morgan are recognizing that
autism is a subject for the workplace. Whether it is
assisting families of their employees or helping
employ those on the spectrum, J.P Morgan wants
to help with these efforts.

ALL THROUGH THIS I HAD A GREAT GROUP OF
FRIENDS AND SUPPORT THAT HELPED ME
ALONG THE WAY AFTER THE BREAKUP
OCCURRED…

Thanks for your support it means the world to me!

PART II: AUTISM AND FALLING IN LOVE

When many people think of autism, they don't often think of autism and love in the same conversation. Growing up I wasn't sure if I would ever be able to find a girlfriend due to my issues with communication. I can now say today I've had several outstanding girlfriends and each one has taught me valuable lessons that I'll take with me for the rest of my life.

When I talk to families with children and adults on the autism spectrum this is usually one of the big subjects, but also one of the most sensitive. How does someone on the spectrum even go about having a relationship while many neurotypicals today cannot? It's a difficult road with no clear answer.

As I mentioned briefly in the introduction of this book, as much as I wanted to share about the one that got away, I wanted to also use this as a vehicle to start a larger conversation about autism and relationships. There are so many stigmas out there that individuals with autism are not able to be in relationships and those with autism not being able to feel love. I'm writing this book to tell you that this couldn't be further from the truth.

Looking back at my experiences, many of my problems in relationships have been due to "social awkwardness." The social awkwardness could be attributed to many factors, but for me it was always based on "small talk" and "mind blindness." With small talk, many times (especially when I was younger) I couldn't hold a conversation, making any type of interaction awkward in the sense of the silence and long pauses involved. The only way I would be able to keep a conversation going was to change the subject randomly to something that was of interest to me (such as basketball). This was hard because while I did have friends who play and like basketball, for instance, it's not something you want to hear about 24/7.

How do you make strides in conversation without having the capabilities of conversation?

Relationships and love **_are_** possible for those on the spectrum. The spectrum is very wide, meaning that some may never be interested in that type of connection with someone else. If you've met one person with autism you've met one person with autism. People such as the leading autism advocate we have in Temple Grandin says that "the part of other people that has emotional relationships is not part of me," and she has neither married nor expressed any interest in a romantic relationship, and she is one of the most high functioning individuals with autism out there.

Convincing this to my mentees is a much more challenging task. As a mentor for high school students with autism, they often discuss their difficulties with trying to find common interests with their peers let alone trying to find a partner. For many it is hard to engage with other individuals because of social difficulties but I've also seen a lack of even attempting a relationship due to the possible pain of being hurt. For many with autism they have a heightened level of sensitivity when it comes to these issues, which makes it highly justifiable.

Ever since I started speaking as a self-advocate and have been getting my name more noticed in the autism community, it actually has opened me up to more dates. Being able to speak to crowds has built up my confidence to be able to be more social and be more willing to open myself up to people.

Here are some key areas of focus that I'd like to share with you on autism and relationships...

Mind Blindness

Mind blindness, which is typically known as the inability to develop an awareness of what another person is thinking, made for some difficult scenarios for me. The inability to express empathy and to do this, to "put myself in the shoes of another," limited my understanding of others, and made it difficult to develop anything but basic friendships/relationships. People are very complex and reading them—not only from a relationship standpoint but to advance in life, whether it's through school, employment, on a professional level, is a necessary skill.

There are different names for this theory including "Mind Blindness" and "Tunnel Vision." This has led some of my peers to believe that I'm self-centered, and that regardless of what I'm doing, it's about me and everyone else has to live with it (which is it farthest from the truth because I feel passionately about other people's feelings).

On the other hand, these experiences glaringly pointed out, that although I have raised the awareness of what autism is, and put a face on what someone with autism looks like, many people have no clue of what it entails or how it manifests or affects many in our community. I've never used my disability as a scapegoat for whatever tendencies I have gone through but what do you do?

Follow my own advice… ***Autism is never a disability unless you let it become one***. I take criticism as an indication of what I could work on to become stronger as a person, but in this situation I've never felt so blind.

I also was blindsided by the break up. I never expected it to happen the way it did. For someone who spent two decades trying to work on communicating to have all communication end abruptly was disconcerting. Facing problems and working through them has been something I've always done and to not have the opportunity to define the problem and have an opportunity to come up with a solution was traumatic for me.

Intimacy

There are still many young adults on the autism spectrum who are never told about sex. It baffles me. Sexual education and avoiding that confusion among those trying to have relationships is imperative.

My own experiences with sex are complex because when I was a kid I had severe sensory integration difficulties. Because of that I didn't like to be touched as a kid. Now I love being affectionate but in relationships I've had a difficulty finding the right balance.

One of the leading experts we have in the conversation of autism is someone I call a dear friend in Amy Gravino. Amy, who lives in New Jersey, is a coach for students with autism who are pursuing a post-secondary education. She is also on the communications team for Autism Speaks.

Amy wrote a blog for Autism Speaks titled "I Wanna Hold Your Hand: Getting Intimate with Autism." I'd definitely recommend looking it up if you are interested in learning more about autism and intimacy. In the blog she discusses her experiences with learning how to achieve true intimacy. Amy couldn't have said it better when she said…

"Above all else, intimacy takes work.

Intimacy takes patience, kindness and a whole lot of understanding. There will always be people trying to solve the great mystery of intimacy, and there will always be shelves full of self-help books and angst-filled rock n' roll songs on the subject.

Intimacy challenges neurotypical and non-neurotypical individuals alike, but the difference is that it is actually acknowledged that intimacy is something that neurotypical people want.

Individuals on the autism spectrum often have to take a different road to arrive at the same destination, but our journey is no less valid.

And the first step starts with seeing us as people who have those desires and needs, and who are as capable of understanding and learning intimacy as anyone else."

Like Amy wrote, it all comes down to understanding. The more you can understand your partner and communicate with them on what their needs are the more success you'll have. Having an education of intimacy and being able to continually want to learn about it will keep your relationships strong.

Common Sense

People with autism can be highly intelligent in different fields where they hold a key interest. They can also not understand common things that go on in people's everyday lives. What I've noticed about common sense in regards to autism is that those on the spectrum tend to be very "book smart" and not necessarily as "street smart" if you've ever heard of the expression.

Things in this area tend to get easier as these individuals get older, however it is still a challenge for many today in our community. When things occur like this in relationships, misunderstandings can result and errors can be made that can make things difficult.

I still don't get common sense at times and have used sarcasm after the fact to make up for certain situations where I feel lost. For me it was a cultural issue as well because I never understood what was socially 'normal.'

Common sense comes with practice and being out in the world. It also comes from being social and learning from other's perspectives in the places you inhibit. My advice is for you to branch out as much as possible to learn not only for this reason but for your own personal development.

Love and Understanding

Human beings in nature are unique. In relationships, especially when there are people coming from different backgrounds, they are likely to misunderstand each other. This holds true especially for those dating someone with autism. When someone on the spectrum might say something that seems hurtful, it may or may not have been intended the way you thought.

This holds true to the people in your lives as well. When friends and family seem to have a "group opinion" in the negative about your partner who has autism, you have the insight of knowing that individual better than most to be able to make decisions and be able to change the conversation to make the ones around you understand them better.

I wanted to share an excerpt from this beautiful poem by Martine Stonehouse, a transsexual woman with autism who speaks very articulately about being misunderstood through her diagnosis. The poem is called "An Autistic Android"…

I live on a world, so alien to me, How did I get here? Why am I so different?

Wanting to be like the rest of you, But not knowing how

to fit in with your world.

Your ways and manners are strange to me, And trying to decipher your customs,

There must be other androids like me, from our far away planet called Autism.

It gets lonely on this world called Earth, when its people are so foreign to me.

So, I search this planet constantly, looking for others like me,

To join me in research, as we probe this planet together, relating our findings to each other,

And understanding our logic together

And reassuring for us that someone out there really does care. Is there someone out there?

When it comes to love and understanding my best advice I can give is simple...

Accept that you don't experience life the same way as someone with autism.

Everyone has their own challenges but autism at its whole is a social and communication disorder. Many will have different quirks that are completely unique to the next person you will meet. An understanding that some situations and events may be misunderstood by those on the spectrum is crucial to acknowledge.

Communication (Non-Verbal, Body Language, Social Cues, Etc.)

I have discussed before that communication is the critical issue when it comes to relationships. In order to do that you need to adjust your non-verbal messaging. Make the connection clear with your body language, which could be misunderstood. Things such as communicating tone, pitch, volume, etc. are also of importance.

If you are cognizant of misinterpretations, simply say how you are feeling or thinking at the time. For those of you who have watched the movie 'Hitch' starring Will Smith who plays a "date doctor" who coaches other men on how to pick up girls one quote that stands out to me is...

"Basic Principles - no woman wakes up saying "God, I hope I don't get swept off my feet today!" Now, she might say "This is a really bad time for me," or something like "I just need some space," or my personal favorite, "I'm really into my career right now." You believe that? Neither does she. You know why? 'Cause she's lying to you, that's why. You understand me? Lying! It's not a bad time for her. She doesn't need any space. And she may be into her career, but what she's really saying is

"Uh, get away from me now," or possibly "Try harder, stupid," but which one is it? 60% of all human communication is nonverbal body language; 30% is your tone, so that means 90% of what you're saying ain't coming out of your mouth. Of course she's going to lie to you! She's a nice person! She doesn't want to hurt your feelings! What else she going to say? She doesn't even know you... yet. Luckily, the fact is that just like the rest of us, even a beautiful woman doesn't know what she wants until she sees it, and that's where I come in. My job is to open her eyes. Basic Principles - no matter what, no matter when, no matter who... any man has a chance to sweep any woman off her feet; he just needs the right broom."

The part of this I come back too often is about communication. It's completely accurate that 90% of your communication is not spoken. It's why being open about your thoughts and feelings becomes that more essential especially if you have a tough time interpreting non-verbal communication.

The more you are able to express yourself in a relationship involving someone with autism the better it will end up being.

Women with Autism Spectrum Disorders in Relationships

Although I've never dated any women who have autism, I have had several woman/girls on the spectrum who are friends who have shared their experiences with me in the process of writing this book. I wanted to express my appreciation to them for this. In 2013, I consulted for the motion picture "Jane Wants a Boyfriend" which looks at the life of a woman with autism in her mid-20's trying to find a boyfriend for the first time in New York City. This experience has opened me up to a better understanding of the challenges they go through.

First, the majority of issues that are focused in our autism community today revolve around relationships. There are many girls who may have signs and/or characteristics of autism that are still falling through the cracks. I've seen a stereotype that girls on the autism spectrum have less difficulty with social and communication interaction.

It seems that women have a better chance to be successful in relationships due to the differences on social requirements.

One advocate who does a great job of sharing her experiences is Lindsey Nebeker. She's on the autism spectrum and is married to Dave Hamrick, who also happens to be on the autism spectrum. In 2009, Glamour Magazine did a piece on them titled "They're Autistic-and They're in Love" which I would highly recommend reading for anyone looking to learn more about autism and relationships. In the article it discusses countless issues that those with autism have to deal with when it comes to relationships such as communication.

Another friend, Stephen Shore who is an internationally recognized expert on autism also on the spectrum was quoted in the piece saying, *"I hear a lot of loneliness, sadness and fear among the autistic adults I meet. Without a natural understanding of communication it's much more difficult for people with autism to find and sustain an intimate relationship."*

The writer of the piece in Glamour Magazine, Lynn Harris goes on to say…

Though connecting with others will be a lifelong struggle, Lindsey and Dave have formed a bond that defies their autism. They may sometimes come across as blunt to strangers, but speaking their own minds clearly and directly—just as they did when they moved in together—has helped their relationship. There's none of the "if you have to even ask what's wrong, then forget it" passive-aggressiveness many couples experience, no expectation of mind reading. "People like Lindsey and Dave put so much thought and dedication into making their relationship work," says Diane Twachtman-Cullen, Ph.D., a speech-language expert who specializes in autism and knows the couple well. "Frankly, we could all take a page from their playbook."

Face-To-Face vs. Online Communication

Although I didn't follow the same path, from what I've seen, for those just starting to date for the first time, I highly recommend online dating. Face-to-face communication can be overwhelming for individuals regardless of autism or not. Websites such as Wrongplanet.net, the largest social networking site for individuals with autism is a great place to start your search.

When consulting for young adults on the spectrum this is where I tell them to usually start and work their way to other forms of dating such as speed dating and meeting individuals at public venues. My other recommendations are about using social media effectively to communicate and build a relationship. These tools can be a good way of becoming comfortable with people instead of always hanging out face to face.

In any dating or relationship scenario I always say an equal balance between the two is the best way to go. The downfall of social media and things like texting is that someone with autism may misinterpret different types of messages from the senders.

Keep in mind there must be a balance. We cannot lose our humanity to social media especially for those with autism who have had trouble with communication built into them. In order to be successful, there must be human interaction, face-to-face dialogue and connections in order to move forward into a sustainable relationship. This is the introductory tool but we must move beyond this in order for those with autism to have a meaningful relationship.

How to deal with a breakup

Whenever a breakup occurs for those with an Autism Spectrum Disorder it can feel almost unbearable due to hypersensitivity when it comes to emotions. I've always found investing in projects as the best way to cope when these situations occur. It all varies between different individuals but the best coping mechanisms that you can trigger are those that you have key interests in where your focus can lie.

At the same time you have to make sure you don't bury your emotions. You need time after a breakup to analyze what went wrong and to go through the grieving process. There are five stages of grief when it comes to losing anyone significant in your life and those stages are denial, anger, bargaining, depression and finally, acceptance. Being able to understand this process at the beginning of a breakup is very helpful.

I've always seen social stories as a mechanism to avoid overload. Social stories are used to help explain a situation to someone before they go into it so they are better prepared and can get an idea of what may happen. I'd like to break down these five stages to help those reading come to this understanding...

1. Denial

Anytime you suffer a break up, especially with a partner who you care for, there will be a stage where you try to deny that the situation is actually happening. For those with autism who have difficulties with transition and can find emotional situations unbearable, being in the denial stage can be a way of avoiding an inevitable situation.

2. Anger

Once the reality of the situation occurs, our emotions turn from shock to frustration toward the other individual and (sometimes ourselves) for having to deal with what is going on.

3. Bargaining

Ideally, we would like to remain in control of situations if we can. No one deals well with the feeling of being out of control of a situation. We try to figure out both internally and externally how we can change the outcome of what's happening and finding an acceptable solution for us. For those with autism this can be one of the more problematic areas because of the transition process.

4. Depression

Most in this stage will be in mourning phase. Being upset and sad knowing that it's over can make things difficult but is part of the process. It's important to surround yourself with people during this time to make sure you don't feel alone while also giving yourself time to be by yourself to process your emotions. For those who don't have a great deal of friends and family, seeking professional help can be very therapeutic to help process your thoughts and feelings. These resources include counselors, psychiatrists, psychologists, social workers, autism life coaches, and if you are lucky enough to have friends and family who have had similar experiences, lean on them. Do not go through this alone.

5. Acceptance

When it comes to acceptance, one of the most important things I tell those with autism is to remember is that you're human. We all make mistakes and if a relationship doesn't work out with one person it doesn't mean that they won't find success in the future. You just need to be open to those opportunities. Yes, it is definitely a more complex scenario due to social and communication difficulties that we are experiencing but again there are billions of people out there in the world. Stick to what you enjoy and try social groups and activities to keep yourself busy and if all else fails try online dating.

There is no set time on how long the grieving process will last. Many dating websites today say a normal individual can get over a relationship in about half the time that person was with their partner (So if they were dating for a year then being able to move on in or around 6 months). My response to this is simply: what defines normal? Individuals are unique in who they are and what they are able to go through emotionally so while some will be able to grieve quicker than others the bottom line is acceptance takes time.

Coping with loss is ultimately a deeply personal and singular experience—nobody can help you go through it more easily or understand all the emotions that you're going through. But others can be there for you and help comfort you through this process. The best thing you can do is to allow yourself to feel the grief as it comes.

Some coping techniques during this time include investing in different projects, getting involved with physical activity to relieve stress, and exploring a new hobby. Using Cognitive Behavioral Therapy techniques to deal with anxiety and yoga to learn methods to reduce stress should be explored. I found going to the gym and using melatonin, which is a natural herb, as well as herbal teas helped me sleep.

Being a partner to someone with an Autism Spectrum Disorder

If you've met one person with autism you've met one person with autism. If there was anything I could share when it comes to advice for dating someone with autism that would be it. Don't label anyone any certain way and just make sure you are always communicating with your partner. This is really universal for any relationship but especially for those on the spectrum.

You have to understand that, anyone with any type of disorder is going to have a much more challenging time trying to be in a relationship than someone who is not. This is especially true for someone with autism.

Along with not labeling others, it's crucial to not assume when it comes to thinking what someone with autism is thinking. Many who don't communicate through body language will be more than willing to communicate with you in a conversation if you ask them about something that you are curious about. Most of all, express your thoughts feelings.

Other things like social interaction is important to address when it comes to social gatherings. Make sure to always ask if your partner is comfortable being among others especially at the beginning of a relationship. Try to ease them into larger gatherings slowly if they feel uncomfortable.

If something bothers you, explain why as clearly as you can so they can understand and have an opportunity to fix the situation.

Romance, intimacy and in essence relationships in general can be confusing for those with autism and they can sometimes not understand the issues that are occurring on the surface.

Two movies I recommend watching to further your knowledge of how those with autism interact in relationships would be "Adam" and "Mozart and The Whale" which you can read more about in the resources at the end of this book.

Coming from someone on the other end of this perspective, I can tell you the way to date someone with autism is to always communicate with them on your feelings. People with autism are some of the most truthful and honest individuals you will ever meet. Try to be as open as possible and don't hide your feelings.

So, finally, To the One That Got Away....

I've wanted to swallow my pride countless times now and make sure you know how sorry I am for everything. I'm not perfect but I've always seen you as someone who was perfect for me. I'll always care for you. This is one of the biggest lessons I've ever had to face and now in my career as an advocate, along with spreading autism education and awareness I hope I can share my experiences with people on how to become better partners to their significant others whenever I speak at future events. I've never thought of relationships in many of my talks but now hopefully I can educate and make a bigger impact for those with autism pursuing love from what I've learned not only from losing you but from what I'm doing now to be a better partner for the people I care for.

As for those reading this, when it comes to relationships, I leave falling in love with autism and the topics above for your overall debate. My view on relationships is simple. Whether you are on the spectrum or not, all relationships are hard work. Whether it is within the relationship or not, the best thing you can do for yourself is be who you are and to negate all the negative energy that may come your way. Yes, there is definitely a need to branch out and find what interests you have which can expand the pool of who you may be interested in. We all know the expression; there are many fish in the sea (but not quite as many if you are not looking).

This is where autism and falling in love begins…

PART III: THE NEXT CHAPTER

Autism is a lifelong disorder. More than 500,000 children with autism will become adults with autism in the next decade. For so long the popular image of autism has been focused on children. Now we need to move on to adult related issues.

There are thankfully now so many examples of adults with autism today paving the way for our community. When I was growing up, I didn't have the luxury of being able to hear from many of these individuals.

Many adults with autism will be capable of and looking for relationships on all levels. If you are a person on the spectrum in love or looking to find love I hope these resources are helpful and should be your takeaway from this book. If sharing my experiences can help you find relationships and love, then the book is well worth it.

In the process of writing this book and working on myself I read a great deal of books and have had assistance from the disabled community to better my understanding of autism and relationships. I wanted to thank the following people for their contributions to the field and hope you will use some of them as resources.

Unwritten Rules of Social Relationships by Dr. Temple
Grandin and Sean Barron

Asperger Love by Amy Harmon

Asperger's Syndrome and Sexuality: From Adolescence
through Adulthood – Isabelle Henault

Asperger Syndrome and Long-Term Relationships by
Ashley Stanford

Asperger's in Love: Couple Relationships and Family
Affairs by Maxine Aston

The Other Half of Asperger Syndrome (Autism
Spectrum Disorder): A Guide to Living in an Intimate
Relationship with a Partner who is on the Autism
Spectrum

Sex, Sexuality and the Autism Spectrum by Wendy
Lawson

Adam: The Movie >>
http://www.imdb.com/title/tt1185836/

Jane Wants a Boyfriend:
www.facebook.com/JaneWantsaBoyfriend

Mozart and the Whale >>
http://www.imdb.com/title/tt0392465/?ref_=nv_sr_1

Navigating Love and Autism – NYTimes.com Amy
Harmon

Relating to Someone with High-Functioning Autism: 20
Tips for Partners

http://www.adultaspergerschat.com/2011/05/how-to-love-someone-with-high.html

Times Dispatch: Relationships are challenge for people
with autism spectrum disorders

http://www.timesdispatch.com/entertainment-life/relationships-are-challenging-for-people-with-autism-spectrum-disorders/article_ebc953b0-bcce-5683-b812-9e8aaed9d487.html

Podcast: NPR: Learning to Love, and Be Loved, With Autism

http://www.npr.org/2012/01/18/145405658/learning-to-love-and-be-loved-with-autism

Autism Speaks Blog: Love and Autism: My Progression in Relationships Kerry Magro

http://www.npr.org/2012/01/18/145405658/learning-to-love-and-be-loved-with-autism

5 Tips for Loving Someone with Autism

http://psychcentral.com/blog/archives/2012/05/17/5-tips-for-loving-someone-with-aspergers-syndrome/

On Autism and Falling in Love: To the One That Got Away Kerry Magro

http://themighty.com/2014/11/on-autism-and-falling-in-love-to-the-one-that-got-away/

Asperger's Syndrome and Long Term Relationships

http://www.amazon.com/Asperger-Syndrome-Long-Term-Relationships-Stanford/dp/1843107341

HELPFUL WEBSITES AND AUTISM RELATED ORGANIZATIONS

Autism Speaks- http://www.autismspeaks.org/

Autism Society- http://www.autism-society.org/

Laura Shumaker: SF Gate-
http://blog.sfgate.com/lshumaker/

Lou's Land- http://lous-land.blogspot.com/

Thinking Person's Guide to Autism-
http://www.thinkingautismguide.com/

A Diary of a Mom- http://adiaryofamom.wordpress.com/

ThAutcast- http://thautcast.com/drupal5/

Autism After 16- http://www.autismafter16.com/

A Wish Come Clear- http://awishcomeclear.com/

SQUAG- http://www.squag.com/

John Elder Robison: Look Me in The Eye-
http://jerobison.blogspot.com/

Interactive Autism Network- http://www.ianproject.org/

Wrong Planet- http://www.wrongplanet.net/

Autism with a side of fries-
http://autismwithasideoffries.blogspot.com/

ABOUT THE AUTHOR

Kerry Magro is an award winning national speaker who is on the autism spectrum. A Master's Degree graduate from Seton Hall University, he currently is CEO and Founder of KFM Making a Difference, a non-profit corporation focused on disability issues and advocacy. In 2012 he consulted for the motion picture hit "Joyful Noise" starring Queen Latifah and Dolly Parton. The film earned over 30 million dollars in theaters worldwide. Kerry currently resides in New Jersey and works in New York doing Social Media for Autism Speaks.

DEFINING AUTISM FROM THE HEART

KERRY MAGRO

In July 2013, Kerry released his debut book "Defining Autism From The Heart: From Nonverbal to National Speaker." The book tells the story of Kerry Magro, now a 26-year-old adult who has traveled the country as a National Motivational Speaker. What makes this achievement exceptional is that he was diagnosed with autism at the age of 4 and was largely nonverbal till he was 2 and a half. Today Kerry writes about his experiences on the autism spectrum from the heart to help others overcome obstacles.

Kerry credits most of his progress to the undeniable love of his parents, Robert and Suzanne Mack-Magro. A great deal of his success would not have been possible without their dedication to getting Kerry the best therapies and services possible. Kerry hopes people who read this book will realize that loving yourself for who you are is key to your development. In this book, Kerry discusses the struggles he endured and how he was able to overcome them with the love he received from so many members of his community. Topics include defining your autism, overcoming obstacles, becoming a self-advocate, reflecting on what is important and much, much more. This book is meant for all audiences and does not require an in-depth knowledge of autism to enjoy.

The book became an Amazon Best Seller for Special Need Parenting. You can purchase the book on Amazon here: bit.ly/DefiningAutism

JANE WANTS A BOYFRIEND

ME AND LOUISE LAGACE WHO PLAYS JANE IN THE UPCOMING FILM "JANE WANTS A BOYFRIEND"

I wanted to give a special shutout to the **people** behind the film "Jane Wants a Boyfriend" for having me as a consultant on the film. During the process of the film I got to read the script and give my impressions of one of the characters in the film that has Asperger's Syndrome (Jane) and is trying to find love for the first time.

You can donate to the movie via their Kickstarter page here:
https://www.kickstarter.com/projects/1217475880/jane-wants-a-boyfriend-feature-film?ref=live

MORE ON JANE WANTS A BOYFRIEND

Jane Wants a Boyfriend is a new feature film, inspired by real life events, about a young woman's pursuit of love and the world that didn't see it coming. The story centers around JANE (Louisa Krause), a young costume intern in New York, working on a theater piece starring her older sister BIANCA (Eliza Dushku). Funny, shy, and candid - Jane is living on the Autism spectrum, a woman who faces unique challenges in her everyday ambitions. As the opening night of the play approaches, and Jane goes on some very eye-opening first dates, we learn that - although we've all been dealt our own obstacles, some more challenging than others - at the end of the day we all deserved to be loved

THE GOLDEN DOOR FILM FESTIVAL

The more autism is covered in the media, and serious film the more understanding we can all gain. Your personal experience can be the next documentary. Film festivals all over the country are including autism related topics. Check out some of these films that autism related films that were highlighted at The Golden Door Film Festival in New Jersey...

You can learn more about this event that was sponsored by Bill and Michele Sorvino at www.goldendoorfilmfestival.org

Acceptance – Gene Gallagher - Laura Shapanes

An Art for Expression- Trent Altman

Art is umm. The way to heal - Derrick Small

A Teens Guide to Understanding and Communicating with People with Autism-Alexandra Jackman

Hands to the Sky Catch Them and Their Yours – Kimberly Townes

Just Like You Autism- Jen Greenstreet

Six Letter Word-Lisanne Sartor

The Odd Way Home-Hands to the Sky- Theodore Perkins

HAVE QUESTIONS?

I know there are many within our autism community struggling. For the future I hope to continue writing and helping others accept themselves for who they are. This will be one of my missions in a non-profit I've launched called "KFM Making A Difference."

One way I'm helping right now is through a scholarship program ran through this organization for young adults on the spectrum who are pursuing college called "Making a Difference for Autism Scholarship Program". You can learn more about this by visiting my website at www.kerrymagro.com

CONTACT ME…

If you ever have a question or would just like to chat I frequently respond to people through my fan page on Facebook at…

www.facebook.com/kerrymagro88 and Twitter @Kerrymagro

If you ever have an inquiry or would like to submit a scheduling request to have me speak at your next event please feel free to reach out to me at…

kfmmakingadifference@gmail.com

I already am working on several books, which I will hopefully have out in the next few years! If you ever have a story you want to share don't hesitate to contact me!

BOOK PROCEEDS

I'll be donating the proceeds from the book to Autism Speaks, and the Special Olympics Best Buddies Program.

If you'd like to make a donation to one of these two worthy charities you can learn more about them below…

Autism Speaks: You can donate to them here:
www.autismspeaks.org/donate

Best Buddies: You can donate to them here:
http://www.bestbuddies.org/donate

MORE ON AUTISM SPEAKS

Autism Speaks goal is to change the future for all who struggle with autism spectrum disorders.

We are dedicated to funding global biomedical research into the causes, prevention, treatments and a possible cure for autism. We strive to raise public awareness about autism and its effects on individuals, families, and society: and we work to bring hope to all who deal with the hardships of this disorder. We are committed to raising the funds necessary to support these goals.

Autism Speaks aims to bring the autism community together as one strong voice to urge the government and private sector to listen to our concerns and take action to address this urgent global health crisis. It is our firm belief that, working together, we will find the missing pieces of the puzzle.

MORE ON BEST BUDDIES

Best Buddies mission is to establish a global volunteer movement that creates opportunities for one-to-one friendships, integrated employment and leadership development for people with intellectual and developmental disabilities (IDD).

Their vision is to put Best Buddies out of business.

Their goals are focused on the Best Buddies 2020 Initiative which they created in 2011, with the goal of opening offices in all 50 states, expanding into 100 countries, and impacting three million people with and without IDD worldwide by the end of 2020. The initiative also includes plans to train 4,000 Buddy Ambassadors, develop 1,000 jobs for people with IDD around the world, and increase the number of school-based chapters to 2,500. As a result of these ambitious expansion efforts, Best Buddies hopes to become a household name by the end of 2020.

A SPECIAL THANK YOU

I wanted to give a shout out to our community for all of those individuals who have helped me during the years.

I hope everyone remembers the importance of giving thanks everyday for the things we have. It can sometimes be taken for granted with how fast the world can come and go.

Unfortunately, I was hit by a town car in New York City late one night and, even though I didn't suffer any major injuries, it truly gave me a better perspective on what's important to cherish in our lives.

There were a group of remarkable individuals who deal with the autism community and relationships who I sought out to gain a better perspective and understanding during this time

Dr. Margaret Hertzig, http://weillcornell.org/mehertzig

Dr. Shara Brofman http://www.drsharabrofman.com/

Autism Life Coach Jaclyn Hunt
http://www.asnlifecoach.com

Autism Life Coach Amy Gravino
http://www.amygravino.com/

Special thank you's on the formatting of the book!

**Kate Calabro, M.A. and Jonathan Romberg Esq ,
Seton Hall University**

EPILOGUE

Looking toward the future, my goals stay pretty consistent with what they've been since I started college: I want to help the world become more aware and accepting of individuals with autism. As a self-advocate I plan on continuing my pursuit to help make this happen by speaking around the country on autism and disabilities to anyone who gives me the opportunity to share my voice.

One of my long-term goals is to open myself up to the opportunities to hopefully find love again. I know I have a lot I want to work on myself to become a better partner and one day I hope I can love someone as much as I loved the one I lost. It's taken me awhile to open up my heart but now that I have I don't want to close myself off anymore. No matter how painful it can be to lose someone, the feeling of falling in love with someone like I just did is what I want now and in my future…

I'm looking forward to meeting that person someday
whomever they may be…

20662389R00061